CONTENTS

THE GIFTS OF Christmas

A DEVOTIONAL JOURNEY THROUGH
THE SEASON OF ADVENT

Published by Outreach, Inc., Colorado Springs, CO 80919
www.Outreach.com

ISBN: 9781635101232
Cover Design by Tim Downs
Interior Design by Alexia Garaventa
Written by Jeremy Jones

Printed in the United States of America

INTRODUCTION

This Christmas, share in the magic as we unwrap four of the most important gifts we could ever receive. During the season of Advent, the four weeks leading up to Christmas, we will dive into the meaning of hope, love, joy, and peace. And we will prepare our hearts to celebrate the coming of the ultimate gift, Jesus Christ.

Advent is a season that is officially observed in many churches. The four weeks before Christmas are set aside as a time of expectant waiting and preparation for the celebration of Jesus's birth. The term *advent* is a version of the Latin word that means "coming."

But Advent is not just an extension of Christmas; it is a season that links the past, present, and future. Advent offers us the opportunity to share in the ancient longing for the coming of the Messiah, to celebrate His birth, and to be alert for His second coming.

There are some differences in the way people celebrate Advent. While the core is the same, some of the traditions and practices vary. This book is based on common practices, and we invite you to adapt it to match the traditions of your own church. One of the main traditions of Advent is the lighting of the candles on an Advent wreath. A circular evergreen wreath represents God's unending love for us. And the lighting of five candles throughout the season represents Jesus's coming to a world lost in darkness. "The people walking in darkness have seen a great light; on those living in the land of deep darkness a light has dawned" (Isaiah 9:2). As we light an additional candle each week, we get closer to the arrival of the true Light of the world.

This book contains devotions for each of the thirty days leading up to Christmas. Based around the weekly Advent themes of hope, love, joy, and peace, there are seven devotions for each theme. There is also a devotion for Christmas Eve and one for Christmas Day. In addition, each of the sections contains an introduction page with verses to memorize, a song to sing, and a verse to focus on throughout the week. We encourage you to use these sections as a guide for a weekly lighting of your own Advent wreath. Whether you do this alone, as a family, with friends, or as a small group, taking the time to practice the tradition of the lighting of the candles will add to the richness of your Advent experience. And singing the songs can make the experience especially fun and meaningful if you have kids.

In a season often marked by frenzied busyness, Advent is an opportunity to set aside time to prepare our hearts. The tradition and the devotions in this book are designed to help us place our focus on a far greater story than our own—the story of God's redeeming love for our world.

No matter what the department stores try to tell you, Christmas has not yet arrived. There is value as well as excitement in patient and expectant waiting. May this be a season of wonder for you as you discover the gifts Jesus brings at Christmas: hope, love, joy, and peace.

THE GIFT OF hope

The first Sunday of Advent signifies the hope people felt in their hearts for a Savior to lead them out of dark and hard times. As we begin this season of Advent, we will spend the next seven days unwrapping the gift of hope. In addition to the daily devotions, take time this week to light the first candle in your Advent wreath. Remember the prophecies that were fulfilled in Jesus's coming, express your desires for this season, and place your hope in the Light of the world who was born a baby in Bethlehem and who is coming again.

LEARN

"For to us a child is born, to us a son is given, and the government will be on his shoulders. And he will be called Wonderful Counselor, Mighty God, Everlasting Father, Prince of Peace." —Isaiah 9:6

"We have this hope as an anchor for the soul, firm and secure." —Hebrews 6:19

SING

"Away in a Manger"

FOCUS

"May the God of hope fill you with all joy and peace as you trust in him, so that you may overflow with hope by the power of the Holy Spirit."
—Romans 15:13

1
THE GIFT OF HOPE

Therefore, with minds that are alert and fully sober, set your hope on the grace to be brought to you when Jesus Christ is revealed at his coming.

—1 Peter 1:13

Do you remember the one Christmas gift you hoped for most as a kid? Maybe it was a bike, a doll, a game, or a pet. Whatever it was, can you remember how it felt to be consumed by that one desire? When we hope for something, we think about it, dream about it, and watch for it with longing and expectation. Everything we see reminds us of the focus of our longing. That's what this season of Advent is about— expectant waiting. Not waiting for stuff, but waiting for a person. And this kind of hopeful waiting is not passive but active as we prepare our hearts for the celebration of Jesus's coming into the world.

Your longings have probably changed drastically

since you hoped for that something special under the Christmas tree. But that familiar feeling of longing returns each year as we look to the gift of hope in Jesus—past, present, and future. Our "hope-so" has become a "know-so." We know the story of Jesus's coming to earth, and as Peter said, we set our hope on the grace to be brought to us when Jesus comes again.

Hope is central to our survival as people. When we lose all hope, our life loses meaning and purpose. And hope is central to our faith. Advent is not just about waiting for Christmas. It is also about waiting for the rest of the story—Jesus's second coming to earth. This hope is based on the promises of God and fulfilled in Jesus's birth, death, and resurrection. So we celebrate Jesus's birth, but we also look forward to and trust in the completion of our hope at His second coming.

What do you hope for this season? How can looking at hope as the promises of God fulfilled in Jesus past, present, and future give you new hope? How will that change the way you live this Advent season?

2
PAST HOPE

And again, Isaiah says, "The Root of Jesse will spring up, one who will arise to rule over the nations; in him the Gentiles will hope."

—Romans 15:12

We live in a society of instant gratification. We get impatient waiting for microwaves, airplanes, and high-speed Internet connections. So just think of waiting thousands of years for something! The people of Israel lived an entire history of waiting. In the darkest days of hardship and exile, the Israelites held fast to the bright hope of the promise of a Messiah. Isaiah prophesied, "A shoot will come up from the stump of Jesse; from his roots a Branch will bear fruit. The Spirit of the LORD will rest on him—the Spirit of wisdom and of understanding, the Spirit of counsel and of might, the Spirit of the knowledge and fear of the LORD" (Isaiah 11:1–2). The prophecies gave people hope, and the words of the psalmist David encouraged them (and us) to hold on to hope: "Be strong and take heart, all you who hope in the LORD" (Psalm 31:24).

Can you imagine the expectation that built over such a long time? Hope must have naturally faded for many, and others must have lost hope altogether that the prophecies of a Messiah would come to pass. In the hard moments of life, it was almost too much to hope for. But Jesus did come, and His coming fulfilled the prophecies of the past, not just for the Jews but for the whole world. In the book of Romans, Paul quoted a prophecy from Isaiah: "The Root of Jesse will spring up, one who will arise to rule over the nations; in him the Gentiles will hope" (Romans 15:12). Jesus was a Savior for the whole world—for all who recognized Him as Messiah and worshipped Him as the Son of God, sent to redeem the world.

How does seeing the longtime hope of Israel fulfilled in Jesus the Messiah impact your concept of hope? How can you use this Advent season of waiting to help you worship more fully?

3
PRESENT HOPE

*We have this hope as an anchor for the soul,
firm and secure.*

—Hebrews 6:19

Imagine the worst storm you've ever been in. Lightning flashes, thunder rolls, the wind howls. A storm at sea is even more overwhelming as the waves toss and churn anything in their waters. When a storm hits a ship at sea, the anchor becomes its only hope. Nothing can be done about the wind and waves and rain. There is nothing solid to tether to. But the sea anchor serves to stabilize the boat in bad weather. By increasing the boat's drag through the water, the anchor can keep the boat from turning broadside to the waves and being overwhelmed by them. The anchor allows the boat to weather the storm.

Hebrews 6:19 compares our hope in Jesus to a sea anchor. Hope doesn't change the storms we are facing—the waves are still as big, the rain pelts us just as hard, and the wind still howls just as strong. But hope can hold us firm and secure so that we are not overwhelmed. This is God's promise as we wait for Jesus's coming at Christmas and His second coming on earth. Hope is what we cling to when the storms of life come, knowing that our eternal hope is in the One who controls the wind and waves and that His love for us is greater than anything life can bring.

What storms are you facing in your life? Do you feel secure in hope or overwhelmed by the waves? How can you cling to hope as an anchor amidst the storm?

4
FUTURE HOPE

*Therefore, since we have been justified through
faith, we have peace with God through
our Lord Jesus Christ, through whom we have
gained access by faith into this grace
in which we now stand. And we boast in the hope
of the glory of God. Not only so, but
we also glory in our sufferings, because we know
that suffering produces perseverance;
perseverance, character; and character, hope. And
hope does not put us to shame, because
God's love has been poured out into our hearts
through the Holy Spirit, who has been given to us.*

—Romans 5:1–5

Cliff-hangers—we love them, and we hate them. They drive us crazy and keep us coming back for more. A cliff-hanger is the end of a story that's not really the end. It leaves us in suspense, waiting in eager anticipation for the rest of the story. The makers of the *Star Wars* movies are cliff-hanger geniuses, creating suspense that lasts for years until the next movie releases. People are so caught up in the story that they put on costumes and camp out in lines just to be the first to find out the resolution to the cliff-hanger.

We often think of the arrival of Jesus as the end of the story—and it was the fulfillment of many Old Testament prophecies. But did you know there are many more that have yet to be fulfilled? Yes, Jesus's life was action packed. He was born, lived, died, rose again, and went to be with the Father. But that wasn't the end of the story either. Jesus's story in our world is not yet complete. And the same is true of our hope in Him—the completion of hope, when all things are made right, is yet to come.

We live in the time between. And that is why we still feel suffering, pain, and doubt. But in Romans, Paul told us to glory in our sufferings because they produce perseverance that produces character that produces hope. The focus is on the future. Our hope is rooted in what God has done through Jesus but looks forward to the resolution of the cliff-hanger. And we hold tight because we know that we won't be disappointed by hope given to us by the God of love.

How can focusing on Jesus's coming this Advent season help you hold on to the future hope of the glory of God? How can hope for the future help you face with perseverance the challenges of today?

5
CONFIDENT HOPE

Now faith is confidence in what we hope for and assurance about what we do not see.

—*Hebrews 11:1*

Do you ever wish you could know the future? Maybe not the whole future, but just a glimpse—enough to be confident that everything will be okay. What would you do with that information if you had it? Would it really take less faith to believe and hope if you had a glimpse of things to come? For Mary, the mother of Jesus, she did get a glimpse of her future through the words of the angel Gabriel. And yet, it seems that knowing what would happen required greater faith than not knowing.

Luke 1 tells us that Gabriel appeared to Mary and told her that she would become pregnant and give birth to the Son of God, the Messiah, the Savior of the world. Really? Can you imagine receiving that message? Unbelievable, right? And certainly not a message that would naturally make one confident, hopeful, or assured. Like so many things in our lives, there was still a great deal of unknowns that required faith. Mary didn't know how it would all work out. She didn't get the details or a promise that it would all have a happy ending. But she chose to respond in faith, replying, "I am the Lord's servant. . . . May your word to me be fulfilled" (Luke 1:38).

Mary was not given confidence and assurance so that she could have faith. We often want assurance before faith, but it usually happens the other way around. The book of Hebrews says faith is confidence in what we hope for and assurance about what we do not see. That means we must choose faith, even when we cannot see the result, trusting that God is there working all things for good. The gift of confident hope comes when we place our trust by faith in Jesus Christ.

Where do you feel a lack of confidence and assurance about the unknowns in your life? How can you choose to step out in faith, placing your trust and hope in God for all that you cannot see?

6
PATIENT HOPE

For in this hope we were saved. But hope that is seen is no hope at all. Who hopes for what they already have? But if we hope for what we do not yet have, we wait for it patiently.

—Romans 8:24–25

Were you ever the kid lying in bed on Christmas Eve, listening for reindeer hooves on the roof? Parents everywhere assure their kids that if they are quiet and listen patiently, they'll hear them. The parents are banking on the fact that if their kids lie quietly in a dark room for long enough, they will eventually fall asleep. But the problem is that excited kids are not patient—pajama-clad kids are famous for popping out of bed every two minutes on Christmas Eve yelling, "I hear them! I hear them!" convinced that the reindeer have landed on the roof above.

The whole Christmas season is built on excitement and anticipation, making it a hard time to be patient. Everywhere we look, the lights and music and advertisements remind us that Christmas is coming. Even as adults, patient hope is never easy. The things we wait and hope for this season and throughout the year are bigger—a child to hold in our arms, a friend to be healed, a job to come through. Like kids on Christmas Eve, we are restless and impatient with the things we hope for in life.

But the Bible tells us that true hope looks different. It is not hope *for something* but hope *in someone.* The assurance that in the bigger picture of eternity God is at work helps us to place patient hope in Jesus Christ no matter the season or the circumstances. Sometimes patience is hard because of excitement. Sometimes it is hard because of discouragement. But either way, Paul encouraged us in Romans 8 to wait for the unseen with patience. And Psalm 42:5 encourages the hurting with these words: "Why, my soul, are you downcast? Why so disturbed within me? Put your hope in God, for I will yet praise him, my Savior and my God."

Feeling impatient? Remember these three things as you prepare your heart for Jesus's coming this Advent season: Praise cures hopelessness. Gratitude helps impatience. Worship brings hope.

What are you waiting and hoping for in your life? Are you feeling impatient with God? Why? What are three things you can do today to focus on praise, gratitude, and worship as you wait patiently on Him?

7
SHARING HOPE

May the God of hope fill you with all joy and peace as you trust in him, so that you may overflow with hope by the power of the Holy Spirit.

—*Romans 15:13*

Picture a homeless man lying huddled in a sleeping bag, propped up against the brick wall in a busy downtown area. It's a heartbreaking image. But now picture that the window of the store he leans against is painted with bright colors, depicting a warm fire in a cozy home. The words "Home for the Holidays" are scripted across the window. Suddenly the heartbreaking scene becomes even more stark as we see with clarity how truly far this man is from home.

A similar contrast exists for many of us this season. The displays of happiness and cheer that are meant to warm our hearts can serve to make us feel more alone and hopeless as we compare our reality to the idealism of the season. The reality is that there is a stark contrast between what the season represents and what many people around us are living. For some it is a season of loneliness, grief, and pain. But just as Jesus entered a dark and hurting world, offering hope in a bigger story, we can do the same. Be the difference for someone this season. Share hope with the world around you—not in an artificial way but by showing genuine care and service to others. This sharing of hope can make our waiting during this season an active waiting. And it can help prepare our hearts to welcome the reason for our hope.

Not feeling like you have hope to share? Rest in the promise of Romans 15:13 that it's not up to you—peace, joy, and hope all come from God, who fills us to overflowing by the power of the Holy Spirit. Look for ways to share hope with others this season—not to create an illusion that everything is picture perfect but simply because God has sent His Son and the world is being transformed because of the work He has done.

Think of someone you know who could use hope this season. What is one practical way you can share hope with that person this week?

THE GIFT OF love

The second Sunday of Advent signifies love and reminds us that Jesus was sent to us out of God's great love for us. Unwrap the gift of love over the next seven days. Along with the daily devotions, take time this week to light the second candle in your Advent wreath. Let the reality that God's love came crashing into our world permeate your life this week. Experience the depth of His love and allow that love to overflow to others.

LEARN

"For God so loved the world that he gave his one and only Son, that whoever believes in him shall not perish but have eternal life." —John 3:16

"For I am convinced that neither death nor life, neither angels nor demons, neither the present nor the future, nor any powers, neither height nor depth, nor anything else in all creation, will be able to separate us from the love of God that is in Christ Jesus our Lord." —Romans 8:38–39

SING

"Hark the Herald Angels Sing"

FOCUS

"And I pray that you, being rooted and established in love, may have power, together with all the Lord's holy people, to grasp how wide and long and high and deep is the love of Christ, and to know this love that surpasses knowledge—that you may be filled to the measure of all the fullness of God."
—Ephesians 3:17–19

8
THE GIFT OF LOVE

But the angel said to them, "Do not be afraid. I bring you good news that will cause great joy for all the people. Today in the town of David a Savior has been born to you; he is the Messiah, the Lord. This will be a sign to you: You will find a baby wrapped in cloths and lying in a manger."

—*Luke 2:10–12*

Have you ever stood in total darkness—pitch black, no light pollution, can't see your hand in front of your face—and lit a match? In a literal flash, there is light, hope, warmth, and possibility. Even that small spark on a wooden stick begins to push away the scary, oppressive, overwhelming darkness.

Jesus's arrival on earth was similar. It was accompanied by a magnificent flash. Those angels must have had an incredible glow! But a helpless baby in the humility of an animal pen? That definitely burned small like a tiny, single match—if that. But it was enough to split the darkness in that millisecond when the Messiah entered the world. The Son of God, delivered to humanity as God's greatest gift, brought the spark of holy, perfect, eternal love to each of us. The darkness of despair, sin, oppression, and separation from God was split. And the small match light of that monumental event spread—and continues to spread—into an inferno of love. In Jesus's birth, love lit the way. In His life, love is the way.

What darkness are you facing? Where do you see the spark of God's love in your life? How will you kindle that love today?

9
GOD'S LOVE IN US

This is how God showed his love among us:
He sent his one and only Son into the world that
we might live through him. This is love:
not that we loved God, but that he loved us
and sent his Son as an atoning sacrifice for our
sins. Dear friends, since God so loved us,
we also ought to love one another.

—1 John 4:9–11

What good is a car that never sees the road? Is a state-of-the-art jet airplane that never flies any better than a paper airplane that has sliced through open air? Would the most priceless artifacts in a museum be on display if they had never been used to do something?

In the foreword to the book *Love Does*, Donald Miller wrote, "We don't like to put hands and feet on love. When love is a theory, it's safe, it's free of risk. But love in the brain changes nothing."

A car or airplane is safer parked, but what good is it? Each is created for motion and transport—for action. Love is the same. And love in the hands and feet changes everything.

God put hands and feet on His love. He took action. He poured out love in and through the gift of His Son to reach His broken and fallen creation: us. And He calls us to do the same, as He did—toward people. The Christmas season can threaten to choke out our love with its busyness and expectations. But it can also provide natural opportunities to reach out to others with love in action. Let's look for and choose life-giving, love-expressing opportunities today. Let's allow God's love to move us into action.

How does focusing first on God's love change our perspective of the Christmas season? Who do you need to love? What three steps can you take to put love into action this week?

10
AMAZING LOVE

And I pray that you, being rooted and established in love, may have power, together with all the Lord's holy people, to grasp how wide and long and high and deep is the love of Christ, and to know this love that surpasses knowledge—that you may be filled to the measure of all the fullness of God.

—Ephesians 3:17–19

Can you imagine what it must have felt like to be a sailor at the beginning of the Age of Exploration? By that point in history, most educated people understood that the earth was round instead of flat, but no one had ever crossed the ocean. Superstitions surely nagged at more than a few sailors' minds: At some point, were they going to plunge over the side of the world after all? Or even if that wasn't a worry, who knew how far the ocean went? Would it really ever come to an end? They would face many storms and challenges, but those sailors were boldly going to find out one way or another.

Sometimes it takes an unwanted storm or challenge for us to push to a deeper understanding of God's faithful love. But when we are forced to forge further into unknown or unsettling circumstances, we find that God's love extends always further. Maybe the apostle Paul had an ocean in mind when he prayed that Christ followers would "grasp how wide and long and high and deep is the love of Christ."

Advent is a season for rediscovering the coming of our Savior—and for gaining even greater understanding of how wide and long and high and deep His love is for us.

How can you look differently at a current struggle to discover new understanding of God's love? What step can you take to rekindle wonder at the magnitude of Christ's love?

11
PRACTICING GREAT LOVE

*Love is patient, love is kind. It does not envy, it
does not boast, it is not proud. It does not
dishonor others, it is not self-seeking, it is not easily
angered, it keeps no record of wrongs.
Love does not delight in evil but rejoices with the
truth. It always protects, always trusts,
always hopes, always perseveres. Love never fails.
. . . And now these three remain: faith, hope
and love. But the greatest of these is love.*

—1 Corinthians 13:4–8, 13

Herbert and Zelmyra Fisher were married for
eighty-six years, enough to set the Guinness World
Record for the longest marriage. The North
Carolina couple got hitched in 1924 and stayed that
way until his death in 2011. "There isn't any secret.

It was only God that kept us together," Zelmyra told the *AARP Bulletin* that year. But it's safe to say the couple knew a few things about living out His love for each other.

Look closely at the list in 1 Corinthians 13 and we see so many other important characteristics that are wrapped up in love: patience, kindness, humility, grace, forgiveness, strength, loyalty, commitment, determination, vision, perseverance, faithfulness, trust, belief, faith, hope, and even more. Maybe that's why Paul said the greatest trait is love: love encompasses and expresses everything else that is good.

It's wonderful to celebrate stories that have endured the test of time, like the Fishers, but it's also important to remember that great loves like theirs are built day by day, minute by minute. As we hear lots about love during this Advent and Christmas season, let's also remember to look for opportunities to express love in all its other facets through even simple daily expressions—to those closest to us and those with whom we share passing interactions. Let's become practitioners of great, triumphant love one step at a time.

What trying situation can you turn into a simple expression of love? Who today needs a touch of kindness and encouragement? What trait in 1 Corinthians 13 stands out as one you can focus on today?

12
THE NECESSARY INGREDIENT

If I speak in the tongues of men or of angels, but do not have love, I am only a resounding gong or a clanging cymbal. If I have the gift of prophecy and can fathom all mysteries and all knowledge, and if I have a faith that can move mountains, but do not have love, I am nothing. If I give all I possess to the poor and give over my body to hardship that I may boast, but do not have love, I gain nothing.

—1 Corinthians 13:1–3

Love is the necessary ingredient. It's the sugar in the cake. Without it, you might bake something that looks like a cake, but one bite will reveal there is nothing but blandness at best, doughy badness at worst. It's an empty shell. Without love in our lives filling us and fueling us, our greatest actions and efforts are just as hollow.

In other words—and to paraphrase the apostle Paul—if I cure cancer but have no love in my heart, it really doesn't matter. If I forge world peace with no love in my motivation, it does me no good. If I rescue slaves or give millions of dollars to charity or buy the coolest and most expensive Christmas presents, all with no love, my actions are empty.

But pure love, God's love, brings life. Through it, we don't have to cure cancer or solve world peace to touch and change lives. And we can be filled and fulfilled as we live our daily lives. God's pure love sustains and satisfies us—always. It never fails.

Our culture offers a million distractions at this time of year that threaten to run us ragged. Even in our rush to buy gifts and bake cookies and attend celebrations, let's choose to refocus daily on Love Himself and let love fill us as the motivation for all we do.

Where is busyness threatening to squelch love as the motivation of your holiday activities? What is one calendar event you can cut? What is one step you can take today to let your Christmas celebrations be driven by a response and expression of love?

13
NO GREATER POWER

For I am convinced that neither death nor life,
neither angels nor demons, neither the present
nor the future, nor any powers, neither height nor
depth, nor anything else in all creation, will be
able to separate us from the love of God that is in
Christ Jesus our Lord.

—Romans 8:38–39

What's your favorite love song? There are some poignant, tear-jerking masterpieces out there. But the canon of pop love songs also provides some of the sappiest, cheesiest song lyrics in the history of humanity. Many are filled with claims and promises about climbing the highest mountains, crossing the widest seas, or enduring the greatest tests and hardships to prove the truth and depth of our love. That's all well and good. Love should bring out our greatest inspirations and aspirations, and we should do all we can to be and do like God Himself. But as humans, we are destined to fail. At some point, our best efforts to love will fall short. At some point, and probably often, we will let down those we truly love the most.

The good news is that God's love does not and will not fail. There is no greater power in the universe and nothing as perfect. There's nothing you or I can do to change that love or take it away. There is nothing that can defeat it. God's Word is filled with examples and promises of His love for us, but these verses from the book of Romans are especially powerful. Look at the list of what cannot separate us from the love of God. His love is stronger than any superpower nation. It is more vast than the mysteries of the universe. It is more personal and true than our deepest depression or haunting loneliness. Even the greatest finality of our earth—death—is limited, broken, and defeated by the overwhelming power of God's love. May our hearts never stop singing its tune.

What do you think can separate you from God's love? How can you remind yourself throughout the day of the power of God's love for you? Where do you need to allow God's love to bridge the gap to another person?

14
LOVE TO SHARE

We love because he first loved us.

—1 John 4:19

Water in nature is a beautiful, refreshing sight. But have you ever come upon a stagnant pool carpeted by thick green algae? It's not so appealing. Such a scene often happens when water can't circulate. The water might trickle in, but it can't flow out. Contrast that scene with a flowing mountain creek or waterfall. The water leaps and babbles and tumbles joyously onward.

Through the gift of Jesus, God pours love into our world and our hearts. And He calls us to do the same. If we try to hoard His love only for ourselves, it stagnates like that stinky pond. God's idea of love looks more like Niagara Falls: powerful, abundant, relentless, and a force that will sweep you away. Get too close, and you're going in whether you want to or not. That's the abundant life "to the full" Jesus was talking about in John 10:10. And that kind of love demands a response to keep it flowing. That's what John meant when he said, "We love because he first loved us" (1 John 4:19). Because of God's gracious love flowing into us, we can respond with gratitude, sharing a generous, life-giving overflow with other people. Essentially, we can go with His flow. Let's seek to be carried in His currents through Advent and beyond, responding generously with gratitude and offering life-affirming refreshment to others around us.

What three things are you thankful for today? What can you do to express gratitude for them? Where has fear snagged you on the rocks of *yes, but* . . . ? How can diving into God's love carry you beyond that fear?

THE GIFT OF joy

The third Sunday of Advent signifies joy and reminds us of the angels' good news told to the shepherds. We will unwrap the gift of joy over the next seven days. Along with the daily devotions, take time this week to light the third candle in your Advent wreath. Imagine yourself on the hillside where the joyous news was announced by heavenly hosts. As you watch for joy in the world around you during this season, surrender the pain and fear of your life and ask God to fill you with the gift of His joy.

LEARN

"But the angel said to them, 'Do not be afraid. I bring you good news that will cause great joy for all the people. Today in the town of David a Savior has been born to you; he is the Messiah, the Lord.'" —Luke 2:10–11

"Let the heavens rejoice, let the earth be glad; let the sea resound, and all that is in it. Let the fields be jubilant, and everything in them; let all the trees of the forest sing for joy. Let all creation rejoice before the Lord, for he comes." —Psalm 96:11–13

SING

"Joy to the World"

FOCUS

"Though you have not seen him, you love him; and even though you do not see him now, you believe in him and are filled with an inexpressible and glorious joy." —1 Peter 1:8

15
THE GIFT OF JOY

Though you have not seen him, you love him;
and even though you do not see him now,
you believe in him and are filled with an inex-
pressible and glorious joy.

—*1 Peter 1:8*

You know the saying "Good things come in small packages." Well, joy is no exception. What a huge concept for such a small three-letter word. Delight, great pleasure, jubilation, triumph, happiness, gladness, exhilaration, bliss. These are all wrapped up in the word *joy.* And as you unwrap this gift during the third week in Advent, you'll have the opportunity to discover the depth of the joy God offers in His Son. This isn't just a fake, surface-level smile. Joy at the presence of Jesus in our world is deep and abiding.

In fact, Peter called the joy that comes from loving and believing in Jesus "inexpressible and glorious."

Like the other gifts of Christmas, we find our joy not based on our own circumstances or efforts but on the loving work of God in our world through Jesus Christ. In fact, joy can exist right alongside sorrow. Joy doesn't remove or replace sorrow, but it allows us to feel joyful even in the midst of sorrow as we experience pleasure and delight in His majesty, love, grace, death, resurrection, and glory. Like a small package under the tree that we discover holds a precious and wonderful gift, joy can surprise us with its power this season.

Would you describe your feelings about Christmas as "filled with joy"? What step can you take today to focus on the joy that comes from loving and believing in Jesus?

16
JOY STRONGER THAN FEAR

But the angel said to them, "Do not be afraid.
I bring you good news that will cause great joy
for all the people. Today in the town of
David a Savior has been born to you; he is
the Messiah, the Lord."

—*Luke 2:10–11*

The scene is a familiar one in Christmas pageants everywhere: kids dressed in bathrobes representing the shepherds who heard the good news of Jesus's birth from the angels. Maybe it's the bathrobes, maybe it's that we've heard the story so many times, but honestly the shepherds often seem distracted and a bit bored. Yet imagine the terror the shepherds must have felt on that first Christmas—sitting on a dark hillside and suddenly witnessing the arrival of real angels. The Bible doesn't say the shepherds were surprised or vaguely interested; it says they were "terrified" (Luke 2:9). Who were these angels? Where did they come from? What did this mean? But the angel's message to them was "do not be afraid." Instead, the angel brought good news that would cause great joy. Despite the terror the shepherds felt, the angel promised that joy would be stronger than their fear.

Our world is full of fear. A quick read of the headlines is enough to scare us all and to prove that many people today are driven by their fears. But the angel's message to the shepherds is for us as well: "Do not be afraid." As we wait for the arrival of Jesus this Advent season, we can take a long, hard look at our fears and then allow them to be replaced by the joy of the coming of Jesus the King. It is a joy that is stronger than fear.

What are you afraid of? Do you believe your fear can be overtaken by joy as you spend time anticipating and celebrating the arrival of the Savior? Who can you ask to help you surrender your fears?

17
WATCH FOR JOY

When they saw the star, they were overjoyed.
On coming to the house, they saw the child with
his mother Mary, and they bowed down and
worshiped him. Then they opened their
treasures and presented him with gifts of gold,
frankincense and myrrh.

—Matthew 2:10–11

The Bible tells us of wise men who felt joy when they saw a certain star. Known as "Magi from the east" (Matthew 2:1), these men knew what they were looking for. They had been studying the stars probably their whole lives, so they recognized the star that told of a King being born. But knowledge wasn't enough for them. They wanted to experience this world-changing event for themselves, so they followed the star.

There were many people much closer in proximity to Jesus who never even noticed the birth of the Savior of the world. Bethlehem was full of people on the night Jesus was born—most of them Jews from the nation of Israel who had been waiting thousands of years for the Messiah. No one noticed. No one even gave Mary and Joseph a room to stay in. Many were probably in a hurry, busy with their own concerns. They weren't watching for joy. Many others were going about their normal lives and didn't notice anything unusual when the family returned home with a new baby. But these wise men didn't miss this amazing event. They knew what they were looking for, they were overjoyed, and they brought gifts to worship the King.

How often do we miss the joy of Christmas because we aren't watching for it? While we are busy rushing around and going through the motions of the season, we have a nagging wish that we could be filled with joy. We wish every encounter could be like that of the shepherds—where the angels burst through the darkness and announced the good news. We want an encounter that's hard to miss. But it's often in the quiet places where we find Him. Even when we don't notice, He's here offering the gifts of hope, love, joy, and peace. Watch for Him in the unexpected places—not in the flashy decorations or the holiday treats but in the hearts of children, the eyes of the poor, the hands of the elderly.

What is keeping you from experiencing joy this Advent season? What can you add to or cut from your schedule today that will help you take the time to watch for joy?

18
SEASON OF JOY

Restore to me the joy of your salvation and grant me a willing spirit, to sustain me.

—Psalm 51:12

Dr. Seuss's Grinch is the antithesis of joy. Not only did this classic character have no joy, he did his nasty best to take it away from every *Who* down in *Who*-ville who did. But in this modern Christmas tale, there comes the scene of Christmas morning when the *Whos* all gather together, hold hands, and sing just as they always do—but this time without a single tree, decoration, or piece of food for the feast. They love all the trappings of their celebration, but those are not the reason for the celebration. "And what happened, then? Well, in *Who*-ville they say that the *Grinch's* small *heart grew* three sizes that day."

As we wait for Jesus's arrival at Christmas, we expect a season of joy and celebration. But that expectation can often magnify the areas in our lives where we don't feel joyful at all. In fact, sometimes we can feel more like the Grinch in the midst of it all. Joy is a feeling, but it's also a choice. When joy is elusive, we can sharpen our focus on the gift of Jesus—the true reason for and source of our joy. Then we can do like the *Whos*: find people who are also looking to the gift of joy in Jesus this season. Eat together, talk together, worship together, serve together. And ask God, as David did in Psalm 51, to "restore to me the joy of your salvation." Let your joy come from the knowledge that Jesus came and is coming again to bring joy to a broken and hurting world, including our own hearts.

Do you need to have your joy restored today? Ask God to fill you with His gift of joy through Jesus. Paul instructed us in Romans 12:12 to "be joyful in hope, patient in affliction, faithful in prayer." Are there ways you can put these instructions into practice today?

19
JOY IN ALL THINGS

Rejoice in the Lord always.
I will say it again: Rejoice!

—Philippians 4:4

Long-distance runners endure the pain of training because they know that learning to overcome obstacles is making them stronger; they are becoming more like the ultra-runners they want to be. And why do you see runners smiling mile after grueling mile as they endure the pain of exhaustion, injury, and dehydration? Because they know the joy that comes when they cross the finish line.

At the finish line of our lives, we also will be met with the joy of the glory of God. Like runners, we are inspired to continue through the pain, rejoicing in all things, because we know that no matter how hard it gets, our finish line will be filled with joy. But the truth is, we don't have the strength to do this on our own. Notice this verse from Philippians doesn't say rejoice in your circumstances always; it says rejoice in the Lord always. The only way to rejoice in the Lord always is through the fruit of the Spirit. "But the fruit of the Spirit is love, joy, peace, forbearance, kindness, goodness, faithfulness, gentleness and self-control," Paul said in Galatians 5:22–23. We cannot rejoice always by simply putting forth more effort. Joy is a gift, given in the person of Jesus Christ. And when we receive Him and live for the ultimate finish line, we can rejoice even in our pain. This joy is not fake but a steadfast trust in God as our strength and comfort.

So how can you increase joy this season? Don't run after worldly satisfaction, which is temporary. Instead, grow in your knowledge of God so that you can become more like Him. Spend time with Him and with His people. Immerse yourself in His Word and His creation.

In what area of life are you struggling to rejoice? How can you refocus on the eternal finish line to help you experience joy? When this week will you carve out time to spend with God, allowing Him to fill you with His joy?

20
COMPLETE JOY

I have told you this so that my joy may be in you and that your joy may be complete.

—John 15:11

The shape of a triangle has many meanings and interpretations in various religions and cultures. But the shape of a triangle itself is naturally one of completion. Each of the three sides is connected to the other two. If any are separated, the triangle is no longer complete. And so a triangle is one way to look at Jesus's description of making our joy complete.

What comes before John 15:11? What is it that Jesus has told His disciples and us so that His joy would be in us and that our joy would be complete? Verses 9 and 10 speak of a triangle of love and obedience. "As the Father has loved me, so have I loved you. Now remain in my love. If you keep my commands, you will remain in my love, just as I have kept my Father's commands and remain in his love." Jesus found complete joy in absolute obedience to His Father, even to the point of complete surrender and sacrifice on the cross. Hebrews 12:2 says, "For the joy set before him he endured the cross." Our joy is made complete by imitating Christ's love and obedience. If we love Him, we obey Him and our joy is complete. It's a triangle of the Father's love given to Christ, who gave that love to us. And it is our obedience to Jesus, who was obedient to His Father.

Yes, joy is a gift. It is a fruit of the Spirit and cannot be manufactured apart from the Holy Spirit at work in our lives. But Jesus's picture of complete joy also shows us our part. We often hope that joy will just arrive wrapped in a big red bow. But this verse tells us that our joy is made complete when we remain in God's love and obey His commands. In John 15:12 Jesus told His disciples, "My command is this: Love each other as I have loved you." Advent is an opportunity to focus on that triangle of completion as we sacrificially love each other and wait for the arrival of God's gift of joy given to the world in His Son, Jesus.

Where do you struggle with obedience to Jesus's command to love others as He loved us? Who can you love this week as you trust God to make your joy complete?

21
JOY TO THE WORLD

But let all who take refuge in you be glad;
let them ever sing for joy. Spread your protection
over them, that those who love your name
may rejoice in you.

—Psalm 5:11–12

Three hikers were lost in a snowstorm. With the light fading from the sky, they could not see the trail ahead or the way they'd just come. The excitement of adventure was gone, and the fear of the unknown crept in. And then a dim light shone ahead in the distance. Imagine their joy upon seeing that the light came from a small cabin—a place of shelter and protection from the cold.

As we walk through life, God is our refuge and protection. His presence allows us to sing for joy. And we can share that joy with others by being a source of God's protection for them as well. It may be a meal, a blanket, a conversation, or a car ride. It could be a gift, a note, or even a literal place to stay out of the cold. Look for those lost in the storm of life who need a safe place this season. Sharing God's joy with them serves double duty as your joy will likely be increased as well in the process.

How can you help provide a place of refuge and protection for others this season? What will that look like in your school, neighborhood, work, church, life? Ask God to help you share His joy with the world around you this season.

THE
GIFT OF
peace

The fourth Sunday of Advent signifies peace and reminds us that Jesus came to bring peace and goodwill. We will spend the next seven days during this final week of Advent unwrapping the gift of peace. In addition to the daily devotions, take time this week to light the fourth candle in your Advent wreath. In a world that seems to be filled with more violence and chaos than peace, allow God to be your peace. Whatever circumstances you are facing, find rest this week in the

LEARN

"Suddenly a great company of the heavenly host appeared with the angel, praising God and saying, 'Glory to God in the highest heaven, and on earth peace to those on whom his favor rests.'"
—Luke 2:13–14

"Peace I leave with you; my peace I give you. I do not give to you as the world gives. Do not let your hearts be troubled and do not be afraid." —John 14:27

SING

"O Little Town of Bethlehem"

FOCUS

"Now may the Lord of peace himself give you peace at all times and in every way. The Lord be with all of you." —2 Thessalonians 3:16

22
THE GIFT OF PEACE

Suddenly a great company of the heavenly host appeared with the angel, praising God and saying, "Glory to God in the highest heaven, and on earth peace to those on whom his favor rests."

—*Luke 2:13–14*

In the dead of winter, in a conflict that enveloped the world, Christmas carols were sung by opposing groups of soldiers in the trenches of war. Sound impossible? The stories of this very thing from World War I are abundant. In "Silent Night: The Story of the World War I Christmas Truce of 1914," Naina Bajekal reported on these legendary events in *Time* magazine: "On a crisp, clear morning 100 years ago, thousands of British, Belgian and French soldiers put down their rifles, stepped out of their trenches and spent Christmas mingling with their German enemies along the Western front. In the hundred years since, the event has been seen as a kind of miracle, a rare moment of peace just a few months into a war that would eventually claim over 15 million lives."

While this was a momentary truce between individual groups whose countries were still at war, it demonstrates the deep desire within each of us for peace. It is that same desire to see conflict and evil overcome by peace that leads us to the hills outside Bethlehem where the angels announced the arrival of God's peace in our world. It is that same longing that draws us again and again to a stable in Bethlehem where an unlikely Prince of Peace was born—the Son of God who would bring peace to all who believe in His name. And while our peace is limited in this life by the fallen state of the world, we hold to the promise that our joy will be complete when Jesus comes again.

Are there conflicts in your own life that you feel could never be overcome by peace? Will you surrender them this week as you prepare your heart for the coming of God's Son, the Prince of Peace?

23
THE PRINCE
OF PEACE

For to us a child is born, to us a son is given, and the government will be on his shoulders. And he will be called Wonderful Counselor, Mighty God, Everlasting Father, Prince of Peace.

—Isaiah 9:6

Think of the most peaceful place you've ever been—a flowing waterfall, a blooming garden, a silent reading spot, a firelit living room. What makes that place peaceful? Sometimes it is the things that are present in the place, like water, fresh air, or candlelight. But more often we find peace in certain places because of what is not there—loud noises, stressful deadlines, demanding family members, or nagging decisions. So it seems natural to expect that a Prince of Peace would remove everything that isn't peaceful from our world.

During Israel's history of waiting for the Messiah, they came to expect a king who would bring them peace by conquering their enemies. They expected strength and power that would remove the things that oppressed them. But Jesus was and is the Prince of Peace in a different way. Instead of removing unpeaceful things from the world, He promises the gift of His peace in the midst of them. It is a peace *in*, not a peace *from*. Peace is not a feeling; it's a Person.

As we celebrate the coming of the Prince of Peace, we look forward to the future when His peace will be made complete in the world and He will end all conflict, violence, and struggle. But for now, we can rest in His peace. Like baby birds that rest beneath the wings of their mother during a storm, we can rest in His protection even in the midst of the many things that disrupt peace in our world and within our hearts and minds. As we wait expectantly for the Prince of Peace during this Advent season, we wait for One who gave up a place of complete peace in order to come to earth, live among us, and offer us

His peace in the midst of our world. Let us welcome the Prince of Peace—in our cities, neighborhoods, families, and within our own hearts.

Where is your most peaceful place? What makes it peaceful for you? How can you invite Jesus into the pain, chaos, and violence of your world, not just into the peaceful parts of life?

24
PEACE WITH GOD

Therefore, since we have been justified through faith, we have peace with God through our Lord Jesus Christ, through whom we have gained access by faith into this grace in which we now stand.

—Romans 5:1–2

Have you ever noticed which Bible character is typically missing from our Advent stories and Christmas pageants? He shows up in the biblical accounts of Jesus's coming, but we conveniently exclude him. You guessed it: King Herod. Somehow he doesn't fit the family-friendly, peaceful picture of Jesus's coming to earth. Herod was not at peace with God and wanted nothing to do with the peace He offered the world. In fact, that peace threatened everything Herod held on to.

It seems almost ridiculous to be so threatened by a young child that you would order the death of all boys age two and under. But Herod knew enough to know this was no ordinary child. This King of Kings had to be dealt with before He threatened Herod's power. It's not a pretty holiday picture. But perhaps it is one we need to look at more often as we anticipate the coming of Jesus. If we're honest, many of us hold on to things in our lives that are threatened by the power of Jesus. We want to come to the manger, but we don't want to leave behind everything else in order to worship the King. We need to loosen our grasp on our sin in order to receive the grace and forgiveness Jesus brings.

But that is where we find peace—by being justified through faith. Jesus's coming to earth, His death, and His resurrection restored our peace with God, which was lost to sin. God has made a way for us to be at peace with Him. It is His gift to us in Jesus. But we have to let go of our sin and accept His grace by faith.

Are you struggling to make peace with God this Advent season? What about His coming makes you feel threatened? What do you need to let go of and surrender to Him in order to receive the peace He offers through Jesus?

25
PEACE WITH OTHERS

*Make every effort to live in peace
with everyone and to be holy.*

—*Hebrews 12:14*

The Christmas story makes it clear that Jesus's coming is for all people. The parents of Jesus were young and inexperienced. The angels appeared to lowly shepherds. The Magi who came to worship were Gentiles, not from the chosen people of Israel. From the moment of Jesus's arrival, it was clear that in God's sight all divisions among people were gone.

The apostle Paul told us, "For he himself is our peace, who has made the two groups one and has destroyed the barrier, the dividing wall of hostility, by setting aside in his flesh the law with its commands and regulations. His purpose was to create in himself one new humanity out of the two, thus making peace, and in one body to reconcile both of them to God through the cross, by which he put to death their hostility. He came and preached peace to you who were far away and peace to those who were near. For through him we both have access to the Father by one Spirit" (Ephesians 2:14–18).

So why do we spend so much energy focusing on the things that divide? Jesus destroyed that wall, but somehow we keep trying to rebuild it. Despite all of our differences, we share the common need for God's grace. His blood covers us all, and through Him we have access to the Father by one Spirit. The reality of differences in our world is still a struggle. Fear and hatred drive people to hostility that causes them to fight and kill. But as followers of the God who brings peace, we've been instructed to make every effort to live in peace with everyone. Not just the people we like. Not just the people we agree with. Everyone. That is only possible as we submit ourselves to the God of peace and allow Him to provide reconciliation in place of the dividing wall of hostility.

Is there someone you need to make peace with? What effort can you make this week to go beyond the dividing wall and live at peace with that person?

26
PEACE BEYOND UNDERSTANDING

Do not be anxious about anything, but in every situation, by prayer and petition, with thanksgiving, present your requests to God. And the peace of God, which transcends all understanding, will guard your hearts and your minds in Christ Jesus.

—Philippians 4:6–7

Do you remember being afraid of the dark? Familiar, safe places like your bedroom or the basement could seem overwhelmingly scary when the lights were out. Furniture became monsters, and curtains blowing in the breeze became ghosts. It's easy to dismiss the fear in children, but in the moment nothing is more real. Yet isn't it amazing how holding the hand of a parent, sibling, or friend can change everything for a child who is afraid? Really, nothing has changed, but suddenly the child has the courage to face the darkness. It doesn't make sense, but that comforting presence brings peace.

What are you afraid of now? What are the grown-up monsters that cause you to be anxious? Paul told us that when we feel anxious in any situation, we are to go to God in prayer. But this isn't a formula for getting rid of anxiety. There is no guarantee that when we pray with thanksgiving, our worries will go away. That isn't the point. In fact, the point is actually in the four words that precede this passage. The end of Philippians 4:5 says, "The Lord is near." When we miss that truth, we miss the whole meaning of this passage. Like a child who is given courage through the presence of someone they trust, we can experience peace as we draw near to God. Like a hand in the darkness, God's presence gives us peace that doesn't make sense in the circumstances. Nothing has changed—but everything is different. His presence gives us a peace that is beyond understanding.

What are you anxious about this Advent season? What are some ways you can remind yourself that God is near, His hand outstretched, offering to guard your heart with His peace?

27
PEACE IN TROUBLE

*I have told you these things, so that in me you
may have peace. In this world you will have trouble. But take heart! I have overcome the world.*

—*John 16:33*

Suspenseful movies or books keep us on the edge
of our seats. But even the best stories rely on the
unknown to keep us in a state of fear and suspense.
Have you ever watched a movie after the ending was
given away? You may still enjoy it, it will probably
still be exciting, but knowing the ending just takes
the edge off. The intensity of emotions is not the
same when you already know what happens. In a
film or book, that's not so good—nobody wants the
story spoiled. But in life, knowing the ending can
bring peace.

And guess what? We do know the end of the story! Spoiler alert: Jesus has overcome the world. We

don't know all the details of what life will hold for us, but ultimately we know that God is in control, has conquered sin and death, and will make all things right when Jesus comes again. Satan loves to cause us to question this: *Are we sure that's how things end? But what about all the pain and suffering before then?* These questions and the realities of life are hard. In John 16 Jesus said that, without question, in this world we will have trouble. Life won't be easy. But our courage and peace come from knowing the One who wrote the story. The One who is both the beginning and the end. The One who has overcome the world and offers us His peace.

Do you believe in the end of the story? How can knowing the ending give you peace in the trouble you face today?

28
PASSING THE PEACE

Peace I leave with you; my peace I give you. I do not give to you as the world gives. Do not let your hearts be troubled and do not be afraid.

—*John 14:27*

Many churches include a tradition in worship called the passing of the peace. Even those that no longer call it that usually include a time of greeting those around you. However, what was started as an opportunity to truly connect with and share the peace of God has sometimes become commonplace, awkward, and empty. Our "pass the peace" has become more like "pass the peas."

But there is so much more to sharing the peace of God with one another. The Hebrew greeting *shalom* is a word that does mean peace but also so much more. It is much more active than the English word and includes completeness, wholeness, health, welfare, safety, tranquility, prosperity, fullness, rest, and harmony. That is what we offer to one another when we are truly passing on the peace of Christ. It requires more than a greeting; it requires getting to know the situations and needs of the people around us and then doing what we can to help them experience peace. When we wish peace to those around us this Advent season, are we really extending God's peace or just giving a shallow word of encouragement that the craziness will be over soon and we'll all return to normal life? Jesus didn't come for that. He came for radical transformation.

In some of Jesus's final teachings to His disciples before He was betrayed and crucified, Jesus gave them His peace. He made sure they knew that He did not give it as the world gives. The peace the world seeks and offers is a temporary one based on avoidance of anything that disrupts our lives. But the peace of Jesus is a deep and lasting peace that endures and transforms everything. Because of His peace we can surrender our anxiety and fear and experience rest as we prepare to celebrate His birth.

Is your heart troubled? Do you feel afraid? How can you surrender those areas to God's peace? How will you genuinely share the peace of God with others this Christmas?

LEARN

"'She will give birth to a son, and you are to give him the name Jesus, because he will save his people from their sins.' All this took place to fulfill what the Lord had said through the prophet: 'The virgin will conceive and give birth to a son, and they will call him Immanuel' (which means 'God with us')."
—Matthew 1:21–23

"Every good and perfect gift is from above, coming down from the Father of the heavenly lights, who does not change like shifting shadows." —James 1:17

SING

"Silent Night" (as well as all the other carols from each of the weeks in Advent)

FOCUS

"The Word became flesh and made his dwelling among us. We have seen his glory, the glory of the one and only Son, who came from the Father, full of

THE GIFT OF Jesus

The fifth and final candle of Advent represents Christ. This candle signifies the gift God gave us in the baby Jesus, His Son, the Savior of the world. Jesus is truly the ultimate gift and the source of all the other gifts—hope, love, joy, and peace. Celebrate the birth of Jesus! The waiting is almost over; the Messiah is coming. And even as we celebrate His arrival in our world, our anticipation grows, and we continue to live with longing and expectation for His second coming when His work will be complete and all the world will be reconciled to Him. Yet even now on the eve and day of Christmas, we rejoice. Christ has come! He will come again!